Collins

INTERNATIONAL PRIMARY ENGLISH

Student's Book 2

William Collins' dream of knowledge for all began with the publication of his first book in 1819.
A self-educated mill worker, he not only enriched millions of lives, but also founded a flourishing
publishing house. Today, staying true to this spirit, Collins books are packed with inspiration,
innovation and practical expertise. They place you at the centre of a world of possibility and give
you exactly what you need to explore it.

Collins. Freedom to teach.

An imprint of HarperCollins*Publishers*
The News Building
1 London Bridge Street
London SE1 9GF

browse the complete Collins catalogue at
www.collins.co.uk

ISBN 978-0-00-814763-1

Joyce Vallar asserts her moral rights to be identified as the author of this work.

British Library Cataloguing in Publication Data
A catalogue record for this publication is available from the British Library.

Publisher Celia Wigley
Publishing manager Karen Jamieson
Commissioning editor Lucy Cooper
Series editor Karen Morrison
Managing editor Caroline Green
Editor Amanda Redstone
Project managed by Emily Hooton and Karen Williams
Edited by Karen Williams
Proofread by Gaynor Spry
Cover design by Amparo Barrera
Cover artwork by David Roberts
Internal design by Ken Vail Graphic Design
Typesetting by Ken Vail Graphic Design and Jouve India Private Limited
Illustrations by Ken Vail Graphic Design, Advocate Art and Beehive Illustrations
Production by Robin Forrester

Printed and bound by Grafica Veneta S. P. A.

Contents

1 Fun and games

Listen to the instructions before you read the story.

Jodie the Juggler

1 Jodie loved juggling. He juggled with his socks.

He juggled with his shoes.

He juggled with three oranges and ...

2 ... he broke a cup.
"Jodie," Mum said, "go outside and play football."
Jodie didn't want to play football.
He wanted to juggle.

3 He went outside and juggled with three flowerpots and ...

... the flower pots broke!
Mum yelled, "JODIE, STOP JUGGLING!"

Read aloud.　1

4 Jodie went to Asif's flat.

5 Jodie showed Asif how to juggle.
They juggled with Asif's socks.
They juggled with Asif's shoes.
They juggled with
three apples and ...

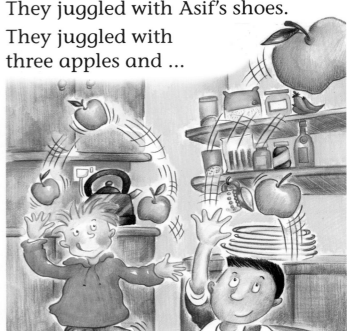

6

... they broke a plate.

7 "Boys," said Asif's dad, "go outside
and play football."
Jodie didn't want to play football.
He wanted to juggle.

Read aloud.

8 Jodie went back down to his own flat. Mum was in the kitchen making a cake.

"No juggling!" said Mum, as Jodie picked up three eggs. But it was too late. The eggs broke!

9 "Jodie," sighed Mum, "we're going to the park to play football NOW!"
Mum carried the football. Jodie wanted to juggle.

10 Dom, Sue and Ash were in the park. They ran over to Jodie.

"Can we borrow your football?" They asked.

"Yes," said Jodie. "I don't like football. But I'll try one kick first."

11 He took the ball from Mum and kicked it as hard as he could.
Up went the ball, up and up and up.

12 Down came the ball,
down and down
and down ...

CRASH!

... it smashed some glass!

DANGER KEEP OUT!

Due For Demolition

13 "BRILLIANT kick!" gasped Darren.
"A golden goal!" yelled Ash.
"You're a STAR!" cried Sue.
"Jodie," said Mum firmly, "we're going home."

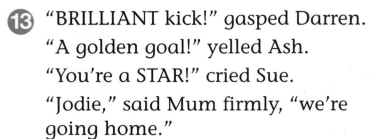

WOW!

WOW!

WOW!

14 Mum and Jodie walked home slowly.

"Sorry, Mum," Jodie said quietly.
"Lucky that man gave us our ball back."

Mum said, "Maybe juggling is a good idea. I'll make you some juggling balls."

15 Jodie looked at her and smiled a huge smile.

"I don't want to juggle anymore," he said.
"I want to play football!"

Oh no!

Reading and understanding

1 **How well did you read? Answer these questions.**

- What did Jodie like doing?
- What did Jodie's mother want him to do?
- What is Jodie's friend's name?
- Where did Jodie's mother take him?
- Who did Jodie meet in the park?

2 **Jodie's friends were very happy with him. Copy the sentences that tell you this.**

- They walked away.
- They smiled at Jodie.
- They had angry faces.
- They said nice things about him.
- They stood beside him.

Listening and speaking

Work in pairs. Talk about the questions.

1 How was Jodie's mother feeling?

2 Why was she feeling that way?

Reading and writing

1 **Read the sentences from the story. Who said each sentence?**

> Dom   Jodie   Ash   Asif's dad   Mum   Sue

- "Jodie, stop juggling." ~Mum
- "Boys, go outside and play football." dad
- "Jodie, we're going to the park to play." mum
- "I don't like football." Jodie
- "BRILLIANT kick!" Darren
- "A golden goal!" Ash
- "You're a star!" Sue
- "Jodie, we're going home."
- "I don't want to juggle any more. I want to play football!" mum Jodie

Hello Jodie, Come on in.

2 **Draw a picture of Jodie and the man in the picture on page 12 after the glass was smashed. What do you think they said to each other?**

3 **Work in pairs. Act out what Jodie and the man said to each other.**

A compound word is made by combining two shorter words.

'Football' is a compound word.

foot + ball = football

1 **Join the words on the left with words on the right to make compound words. Write the compound words.**

tea	butter
super	hand
up	fire
see	for
grand	

market	writing
saw	mother
fly	stairs
work	spoon
get	

2 **Use the words in the box to complete the sentences.**

don't could some

- He kicked the ball as hard as he _____.
- It smashed _____ glass.
- I _____ like football.

Reading and writing

1 **Write a list of the things that Jodie juggled with.**

2 **Write a list of things that Jodie broke.**

Remember

Items in a list are normally written one below the other.

3 **Write the things that Jodie did in the correct order.**

- He went to Asif's flat
- He juggled with oranges.
- He broke a plate.
- He broke the flower pots.
- He juggled with apples.

Listening and speaking

Work in pairs. Talk about what happened in the next part of the story.

Writing

Write what happened. Start your story with:

Jodie went back ...

1 Before you read the poem, read the title and look at the pictures. What do you think this poem is about?

Janet the Juggler

Janet the juggler
Had jackets galore.
How they jingled and jangled,
Those jackets she wore.

She jiggled and juggled
With jumpers and jeans
And jam-jars and jewels
And five jelly-beans.

2 Read the poem aloud with a partner.

3 Did you enjoy this poem? Tell your group what you liked or did not like about the poem.

Reading and writing

1 **Copy and complete the sentences. Choose from the words above.**

- The door _____ when it opened.
- The rocket _____ into space.
- The pots and pans _____ onto the floor.
- The fire _____ as it burned.
- The girl _____ the horn on the bike.

2 **Draw a picture using each word below. Write a caption for each picture.**

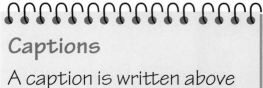

Captions

A caption is written above or below a picture to explain what it shows.

Reading and writing

1 **Write a list of words that could describe the socks in the picture.**

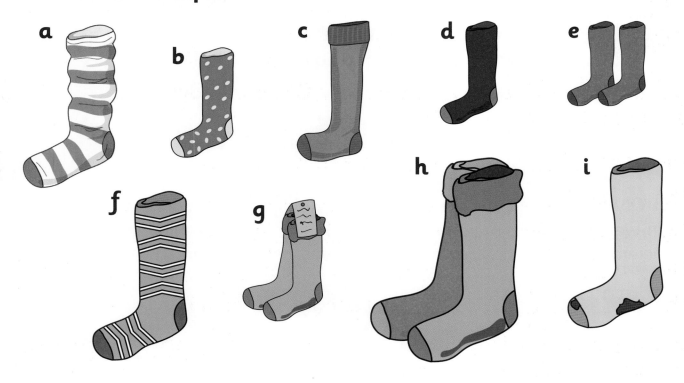

a   b   c   d   e

f   g   h   i

2 **Which of the socks in the picture do you like best? Write a sentence to describe those socks.**

3 **Add words to make the sentences more interesting. Copy the sentences.**

- Jodie juggled with his _____ shoes.

- "A _____ kick!" gasped Dom.

- Mum was making a _____ cake.

- "A _____ goal!" yelled Ash.

- Jodie juggled with Asif's _____ socks.

2 The Olympics

Reading

Skim read the information about the
Olympic Games on the following pages.

The Olympic Games

The First Olympic Games

The first Olympic games were held in 776BC in Olympia in Greece.
Only men were allowed to compete. Legend has it that the winners of
these ancient games were crowned with leaves from an olive tree.

The Modern Olympics

The first modern Olympic Games
took place in 1896 and since then 30
summer Olympic Games have been
held and 21 winter Olympic Games.

The summer Olympics are always held
in a leap year.

The Olympic Rings and Flag

The five Olympic rings represent
the five continents of the world –
America, Europe, Asia, Africa and
Australia – and the coming together of
athletes from different countries.

The six colours of the Olympic flag – red, yellow, green, blue,
black and white appear on national flags around the world.

The Olympic Torch

The torch relay and the lighting of the torch in the stadium at the opening ceremony is said to keep the Olympic spirit alive all around the world.

Olympic Medals

After their events, the winners stand on the podium to get their medals. The flags of the medallists' countries are flown at the medal ceremony. The first place winner gets a gold medal, the second place gets a silver medal and the third place gets a bronze medal.

Olympic Sports

There are many different sporting events in the Olympics. Sports in the summer Olympics are different from the ones in the winter Olympics.

skiing

gymnastics

archery

Recent Olympic Games

The summer Olympic Games in 2012 were held in London in the United Kingdom from July 27th to August 12th. London previously hosted the Games in 1908 and 1948, making 2012 the third time for London.

The 2012 London Olympic Games were watched by over 80,000 spectators inside the stadium and by an estimated television audience of 900 million people worldwide.

Reading and writing

1 **Read through the information on the Olympics again. Find the answers to these questions.**

- Where were the first Olympic Games held?
- What prize did the winner of the ancient games get?
- When were the first modern Olympics?

- Which five continents do the Olympic rings represent?
- What colours make up the Olympic flag?

2 **Draw and label the flag of the country that you live in.**

3 **Find out about a flag of another country. Draw and label it.**

Speaking and writing

1 **The modern games have their own website to advertise the games. Work in pairs. Talk about what an ancient Olympic poster or advertisement might have looked like.**

2 **Make a list of the information that might have been on an ancient Olympic advertisement.**

3 **Design an advertisement for the first Olympic Games.**

Find answers to questions. Features of text types.

Write what is happening in each picture.
The words in the box will help you.

podium medal	javelin	high jumper
relay baton	diving board	starting line

1

2

3

4

5

6

Reading and writing

1 **Skim read the information text on pages 12 and 13 again to answer the questions.**

- When were the Olympic Games last held in London?
- What date did they start?
- What date did they finish?
- How many times has London hosted the Olympic Games?
- In what years have the Olympic Games been hosted in London?
- How many people watched the Olympic Games at the Olympic Stadium in London?

2 **Work in pairs. Talk about the information that you get from this poster for athletics at the Olympic Games.**

3 **Check that you know the meanings of the words 'venue' and 'competitors'.**

4 **Design a poster to give information about a sports event at your school.**

Athletics
at the Olympics Games

Venue	Olympic stadium
Dates	August 1st to August 14th
Competitors	2231 (1160 men, 1071 women)

Olympic medal winners

Women's 100 metres		
🥇	Shelley-Ann Fraser-Pryce	Jam
🥈	Carmelita Jeter	USA
🥉	Veronica Campbell-Brown	Jam

Men's 100 metres		
🥇	Usain Bolt	Jam
🥈	Yohan Blake	Jam
🥉	Justin Gatlin	USA

Women's 100 metre hurdles		
🥇	Sally Pearson	Aus
🥈	Dawn Harper	USA
🥉	Kellie Wells	USA

Men's 110 metre hurdles		
🥇	Aries Merritt	USA
🥈	Jason Richardson	USA
🥉	Hansle Parchment	Jam

Women's 5000 metres		
🥇	Meseret Defar Tola	Eth
🥈	Vivian Jepkemoi Cheruiyot	Ken
🥉	Tirunesh Dibaba Kenene	Eth

Men's 5000 metres		
🥇	Mo Farah	GBR
🥈	Dejen Gebremeskel	Eth
🥉	Thomas Pkemei Longosiwa	Ken

1 **Write the name of the country for each flag.**

a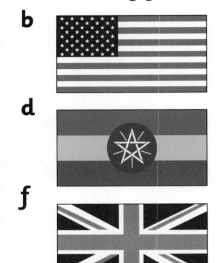

b

c

d

e

f

| USA |
| Jamaica |
| Ethiopia |
| Great Britain |
| Australia |
| Kenya |

2 **Read the table on page 17 to answer the questions.**

- Who won the women's 100 metres?
- Who won the silver medal in the women's 100 metres hurdles?
- List the names of the winners of the men's hurdles.
- Who won gold in the men's 100 metres?
- In which race did Great Britain win a gold medal?
- In which race did Australia win a gold medal?
- Who won a bronze medal in the women's 5000 metres?

Reading and writing

① Answer the questions

- Who won the women's 100 metre hurdles?
- What was her time?
- Who ran the race in 12.37 seconds?
- Which country did the bronze medallist come from?

Women's 100 metre hurdles			
1 Sally Pearson	12.35 seconds	Aus	⚑
2 Dawn Harper	12.37 seconds	USA	⚑
3 Kellie Wells	12.48 seconds	USA	⚑

② Choose one of the hurdlers and imagine you are writing in your diary after the event.

It was such an important occasion and you don't want to forget anything.

Think about:

- how you felt before the race as you waited at the starting line
- how you felt after the race
- the crowd's reaction
- your time
- how you felt on the podium.

•• Usain Bolt ••

Usain Bolt was born in Jamaica on 21 August 1986. He is a sprinter and holds the world record for the 100 and 200 metre events. He is so fast he has been given the nickname 'Lightning Bolt'.

He won three gold medals and broke three world records at the 2008 Olympic Games in Beijing, China.

He defended all three titles at the 2012 Olympic Games in London, by winning gold in the 100m, 200m and 4 × 100m relay.

❶ **Answer the questions.**

- When was Usain Bolt born?
- Where was Usain Bolt born?
- What is Usain Bolt's nickname?
- How many gold medals did he win at the 2008 Beijing Olympics?
- How many gold medals did he win at the 2012 London Olympics?

❷ **Write a short article for your local newspaper about Usain Bolt's win at the 2012 London Olympics.**

- Think of a good headline for your article.

3 What's for lunch?

You are going to read a play. Before you read it, look at the pictures and discuss the questions.

- What is the play about?
- Where does the play take place?
- Who are the characters in the play?

Worm Looks for Lunch

The play begins on a piece of ground under a large tree.

Worm wiggles out of the ground.

 Storyteller: One day, Worm wiggled out of the ground.

 Worm: (crossly)
Earth! Earth! Earth!

I'm fed up with earth for lunch!

I'm going to look for some new food.

Worm wiggles over the grass towards Rabbit.

 Storyteller: Worm wiggled over the grass.

 Rabbit: Hello, Worm.

Worm: Hello. Who are you?

❸

 Rabbit: I'm a rabbit.

 Worm: And what do you like to eat?

 Rabbit: I like eating grass.

 Worm: I think I'll try some grass.

 Storyteller: So Worm tried some grass.

❹

 Worm: (pulling a face) No, I don't like grass. It's too chewy.

Worm meets Deer under the tree.

❺

 Storyteller: Worm wiggled along to a tree.

 Deer: Hello, Worm.

 Worm: Hello. Who are you?

 Deer: I'm a deer.

 Worm: And what do you like to eat?

❻

 Deer: I like eating bark.

 Worm: I think I'll try some bark.

 Storyteller: So Worm tried some bark.

 Worm: (pulling a face) No, I don't like bark. It's too hard.

❼

Worm wiggles up the tree.

 Storyteller: Worm wiggled up the tree.

 Beetle: Hello, Worm.

 Worm: Hello. Who are you?

 Beetle: I'm a beetle.

 Worm: And what do you like to eat?

 Beetle: I like eating leaves.

 Worm: I think I'll try a leaf.

 Storyteller: So Worm tried a leaf.

 Worm: (pulling a face) No, I don't like this leaf. It's too dry.

❽

Worm is wiggling along a twig.
Bird sees him.

 Storyteller: Worm wiggled along a twig.

 Bird: Hello, Worm.

 Worm: Hello. Who are you?

 Bird: I'm a bird.

 Worm: And what do you like to eat?

 Bird: Let's think. I like eating beetles.

❾

❿

⑪

 Worm: (looking upset)
Oh, no! Beetle! Beetle!
Run and hide, or else
Bird will eat you!

 Bird: No, I won't.

 Worm: You won't? Why not?

 Bird: Because there's
something else I like
even better than beetles.

 Worm: What's that?

 Bird: I like eating ... WORMS!

 Worm: (very scared)
Oh, no!

⑫

⑬

⑭

Worm falls off the tree.

 Storyteller: Worm fell off the tree.

He landed on the earth
and wiggled safely
back into the ground.

 Worm: (happily)
Earth! Earth! Earth!
Yum, yum, yum.

Read aloud with accuracy, fluency and expression.

Reading and writing

Order of appearance
This tells you the order in which the characters appeared in the play.

❶ Write a list of the characters in the play. Put them in order of appearance.

❷ Who said it? Write the character's name and what it said.

- "I like eating grass."
- "I like eating beetles."
- "I'm fed up with earth for lunch!"
- "I like eating bark."
- "I like eating leaves."
- "I like eating ... WORMS!"

❸ Join these pairs of sentences using 'and' or 'but'.

- "I'm a rabbit. I like eating grass."
- "I tried some grass. I didn't like it."
- "I am a bird. I like eating beetles."
- "I like eating beetles. I like eating worms even better."

Reading and writing

Remember

Use a capital letter at the beginning and a full stop at the end of each sentence.

1 **Why didn't the worm like eating**

- grass?
- bark?
- leaves?

Write your answers in sentences.

2 **What do you like eating? Make a list of things that you like to eat.**

3 **Choose your favourite food and draw a picture of you eating it.**

4 **Write a caption under the picture.**

5 **Write a list of words that describe food that you like to eat.**

6 **Write a list of words that describe food that you don't like to eat.**

Reading and writing

1 **Copy and complete the sentences. Use the words in the box.**

bitter	hard	sticky	crunchy	sweet	juicy

- A mango has a _____ stone in the centre.
- A lemon has a _____ taste.
- The _____ peach was very ripe.
- The _____ toffee stuck to my teeth.
- Sugar has a _____ taste.
- I like a _____ breakfast cereal.

'Tasty' and 'delicious' are words often used to describe food.

2 **Write two sentences about food. One with the word 'delicious' and one with the word 'tasty'.**

3 **Write two sentences about food that you don't like. Say what the food is and why you don't like it.**

4 **Design a packet for a new breakfast food.**

1 Write the names of the characters in the order that the worm met them.

2 Write what each character ate.

3 Work in pairs. Take turns to imagine you are the worm telling your story.

4 Write your story. You could start your story like this:

When I went looking for food I met ...

Then ...

Next ...

Last of all ...

Structure a story with beginning, middle and end.

1 Read the two poems silently on your own.

2 Which poem do you like best? Tell your partner which poem you prefer and why you like it more than the other one.

Caterpillar

Creepy crawly caterpillar
Looping up and down,
Furry tufts of hair along
Your back of golden brown.

You will soon be wrapped in silk,
Asleep for many a day;
And then, a handsome butterfly,
You'll stretch and fly away.

By Mary Dawson

The Caterpillar

Brown and furry
Caterpillar in a hurry;
Take your walk
To the shady leaf or stalk.

May no toad spy you,
May the little birds pass by you;
Spin and die,
To live again a butterfly.

By Christina Georgina Rosetti

Writing

1 Make a list of all the words the poets used to describe caterpillars.

2 Read the poems again. Find the words that rhyme with each word below.

- 'down' rhymes with ___
- 'die' rhymes with ___
- 'walk' rhymes with ___
- 'day' rhymes with ___

Rhyming words

When the endings of words sound the same, we say the words rhyme.

Spelling

1 **Copy and complete the sentences.**
Use the correct word from the box.

to   too

- It's _____ hard.
- And what do you like _____ eat?
- Worm wiggled along _____ a tree.
- It's _____ hard.
- It's _____ dry.

2 **Look at the pictures. Write the words.**

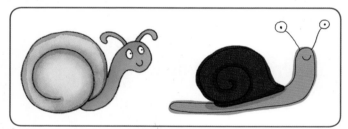

two flags

3 **Copy and complete.**

- It is _____ hot in the sun.
- An owl has _____ wings.
- I went _____ play in the park.
- The box is _____ heavy _____ carry.
- There are _____ cakes left on the plate.

Reading and writing

1 Look at the pictures. Write a word from the box for each picture.

Robbing Hood

A play in three acts

Act 1 In the forest

 Interval

Act 2 Robbing the rich

Act 3 Helping the poor

 The end

Robbing Hood

Coming soon to a theatre near you!

poster   ticket   costumes   programme

2 Design a poster telling people about the performance of the play *Worm Looks for Lunch.*

3 Design a programme for the play.

4 The instructions for 'How to put on a play' are in the wrong order. Write them in the correct order.

- Put on costumes.
- Choose the people to be each character.
- Perform the play.
- Rehearse the play.

4 Kind Emma

Reading and speaking

1 **Look at the pictures. Discuss what you think this story will be about.**

2 **Describe the two characters that you can see in the pictures.**

Kind Emma lived all alone with no one to talk to.

One night, a little voice called,
"Oh, dear Emma, oh!
Where can I go
in the wind and in the snow?"

"Come into my house," said Kind Emma.
She opened the door and a tiny thing scuttled in.
It was almost too small to be seen.

Then the little voice said:
"Oh, dear Emma, oh!
Your fire has burned low
And I shiver so!"

"I'll make the fire glow for you," said Kind Emma,
and she poked the fire.

Read fluently with expression.

Then the little voice said:
"Oh, dear Emma, oh!
I ate long ago.
I need food so!"

"You can share what I have," said Kind Emma.

She put a dish of hot soup and a very small spoon on the table.
The tiny thing stayed hidden. It was afraid to come out.

"Goodnight!" said Kind Emma. She hoped the tiny thing would
come out and eat if she left the room.

Next morning, when Emma awoke …

… the fire burned and the water was hot. Fresh bread was ready.
The floor was scrubbed and the house was tidy and clean.

"Good food and a fire, and someone to
talk to! What more could I want?"
said Kind Emma.
The tiny thing stayed with Kind Emma
for all of the rest of her days.

1 **Read the story.**
Write the names of the
characters in the story.

2 **Choose the correct words to complete the sentences.**
Copy the sentences.

scuttled	lived	stayed	poked	put	was

- Kind Emma _____ all alone.
- A tiny thing _____ in through the door.
- Kind Emma _____ the fire.
- She _____ a dish of hot soup on the table.
- The tiny thing _____ hidden.
- It _____ afraid to come out.

3 **Write a sentence using 'and' to**
tell what Emma did next.

4 **Write the names of the people**
who live in your house.

5 **Write a sentence about your house.**

6 **Write your name and address.**

Reading and writing

1 **Write the answers to these questions. Remember to answer in sentences.**

- Who scuttled in when Emma opened the door?
- What did Emma put on the table?

2 **Write the sentences that tell that Emma was kind.**

- You can share what I have.
- Kind Emma lived all alone.
- I'll make the fire glow for you.
- When I awoke the house was clean.
- Come into my house.

Listening and speaking

Work in pairs. Talk about a time when you were kind to someone.

Writing

1 **Write about a time when you were kind to someone. Remember to tell:**

- the person's name
- whether they were a friend, a relative or someone that you had just met
- what the kind thing was that you did.

2 **Let your partner read your story while you read theirs.**

Reading and writing

1 **Who did these things? Emma or the 'thing'?**

Make two lists. One for Emma and one for the 'thing'.

- opened the door
- scuttled in
- poked the fire
- stayed hidden
- scrubbed the floor
- left the room
- stayed with Kind Emma

2 **Write the verbs from Question 1 in a list.**

3 **Write each word from the first box beside words from the second box that have a similar meaning.**

shiver	scuttle	glow	poke	share

run quickly

push a pointed object into someone or something

shake slightly because you feel cold or ill

shine brightly

divide things

For example: 'share – to divide things'.

Reading and writing

1 **Read the sentences about the story.**
Write 'true', 'false' or 'can't tell' for each one.

- Kind Emma lives alone.
- Kind Emma has a sister.
- Kind Emma has a table in her house.
- Kind Emma lives in a house with no stairs.
- Kind Emma didn't have a fire in the house.
- Kind Emma put a dish of hot soup on the table.
- Kind Emma likes baking cakes.

2 **Copy and complete the sentences.**

unwell	unlock	dislike
unfit	unpack	disobey

- He used a key to _____ the door.
- We had to _____ the suitcase after our holiday.
- The player should not _____ the rules of the game.
- I stayed in bed when I was feeling _____.
- The runner was _____ for the race.
- I _____ some vegetables.

Emma was unhappy.

Reading and writing

1 **Write the names of the days of the week.**

2 **Write two diary pages for Emma. Write the sentences in the correct pages.**

- When I awoke the house was tidy and clean.
- I was lonely.
- A tiny 'thing' came into my house.
- There was fresh bread on the table.
- I gave it a dish of hot soup.
- I said goodnight and went to bed.
- I played 'snakes and ladders' with the 'thing'
- I had someone to talk to.

3 **Think of five things that you do in a school day.**

- Draw each of the five things in order.
- Write a caption under each picture.

Emma's Diary
Monday

Emma's Diary
Tuesday

Sequence of events of a story.

Reading and writing

1 **Write what is happening in each picture.**

2 **What happened next? Complete the story.**

Next morning,
when Emma
awoke ...

3 **Work in pairs. Talk about a different ending for the story.**

4 **Write a different ending for the story.**

Next morning, when Emma awoke ...

Writing

1 Work in pairs. Answer the questions.

- Where did Emma meet the 'thing'?
- How did it feel?
- How did Emma try to help?
- What happened next?

2 Pretend that you met a 'thing'. Work with your partner and plan a story.

Think about:

where you met the 'thing'

↓

what happened when you met

↓

what your 'thing' looked like

↓

how you helped the 'thing'

↓

what happened next.

3 Write your story.

Structure of a familiar story. Plan writing.

5 Animals and us

1 Listen as your teacher reads the first two verses from this poem.

2 Talk about the title of the poem. Why do you think the poet called this poem *Dolphin Ballet*?

Dolphin Ballet

A graceful water weaving dolphin
swirls wakes of gentle waves –
a white, silver blue phantom
shimmering in the noonday sun.

Piercing the surface,
she dances an aquatic ballet
of corkscrew pirouettes
and majestic somersaults.

By Robert Charles Howard

Reading and thinking

This is the title page of the story you are going to read.

1 What type of story is this?

2 What do you think the story will be about?

3 Now read the story on pages 42 to 43.

The
Dolphin King
A folk tale from France

Written by Saviour Pirotta
Illustrated by Fausto Bianchi

The Dolphin King

1 Jean and his friends were fishermen.

Jean said, "I can throw a spear better than any of you."

He hurled his spear at a dolphin.

The animal screamed and dived beneath the waves.

2 Suddenly, a fierce storm blew up and it looked as though the boat might sink.

Then Jean and his friends saw a strange knight rising out of the waves.

The knight shouted, "You nearly killed the dolphin king, and for this you'll all drown!"

Read aloud with increased accuracy, fluency and expression.

3 Jean cried, "No, I alone threw the spear. Take me."

The knight carried Jean down to the bottom of the sea.

There, the dolphin king was waiting.

The knight whispered to Jean, "You must heal him."

4 Gently, Jean removed the spear. He cleaned the wound.

The king opened his eyes and said, "Promise me that you and your friends will never hunt dolphins again."

Jean cried, "I promise."

5 The knight took him back to the boat. The storm had died and Jean's friends were saved.

Reading and writing

1 **Answer the questions.**

- What work did Jean do?
- What did Jean use to catch fish?

2 **Read the story again. Now read the sentences about the story. Answer 'true', 'false' or 'can't tell' for each one.**

- Jean went fishing with his friends.
- Jean went fishing on Monday.
- Jean was boastful.
- Jean's friend hurled his spear.
- Jean's spear hit a dolphin.

3 **Copy the sentence that tells what happened next.**

- The dolphin swam away.
- The dolphin screamed and dived beneath the waves.

4 **Change the word 'beneath' for one of the words in the box.**

The dolphin dived **beneath** the waves.

beside   under   between

5 **Write the new sentence.**

❶ **Copy and complete the sentences. Use the words in the box.**

strange	hurled	heal	fierce	removed	whispered

- Jean _____ his spear at a dolphin.
- Suddenly a _____ storm blew up.
- Jean and his friends saw a _____ knight.
- The knight _____ to Jean, "You must heal him."
- Gently, Jean _____ the spear.

❷ **Write the word that tells you:**

- the storm started very quickly
- Jean was very careful when he removed the spear.

❸ **Write a sentence to tell when the knight shouted.**

❹ **Write a sentence to tell when the knight whispered.**

❺ **Write a sentence with the word 'shouted' and a sentence with the word 'whispered'.**

The knight shouted …   The knight whispered …

Reading and writing

1 Who said it? Write the name.

Jean   the dolphin king   the knight

- "I can throw a spear better than any of you."
- "You nearly killed the dolphin king, and for this you'll all drown!"
- "No, I alone threw the spear. Take me."
- "You must heal him."
- "Promise me that you and your friends will never hunt dolphins again."
- "I promise."

2 Write what happened next in the story.

3 Write the words from the box that describe Jean after the storm blew up.

afraid   brave   honest   fearful   fearless   truthful   dishonest

Listening and talking

Work in pairs. Talk about the questions.

1 Do you think Jean kept his promise?

2 Why you think Jean did this?

Find answers to questions. Vocabulary choices. Attentive listening.

Sounds and spelling

1 **Write the words that end in −ear.**

fear	dear	deal	hear	near
heal	clear	spear	clean	shear

2 **Copy and complete the sentences. Use words from question 1.**

- You can see the fish in the _____ water.
- My house is _____ the school.
- I cannot _____ what you are saying.

3 **Write the words that end in −air.**

chair	chain	fair	hair
stain	stair	pair	pain

4 **Copy and complete the sentences. Use words from question 3.**

- I cannot find a _____ of socks.
- My _____ is needing a cut.
- My _____ is a bit wobbly.

5 **Read the words in the box carefully. Write a sentence for each word.**

far	fair	star	stair

Reading and writing

1 **Read the words below about different types of weather. Write the ones that might happen in a fierce storm.**

gentle breeze   heavy rain   high waves   showers

calm sea   strong winds   bright sunshine   dark clouds

downpours   fluffy clouds   thunder and lightning   blue sky

2 **Write a story about being caught in a storm.**

- Where were you?
- What did you do during the storm?
- What happened after the storm?

3 **Write the types of wind in the correct order of strength.**

gale   hurricane   breeze

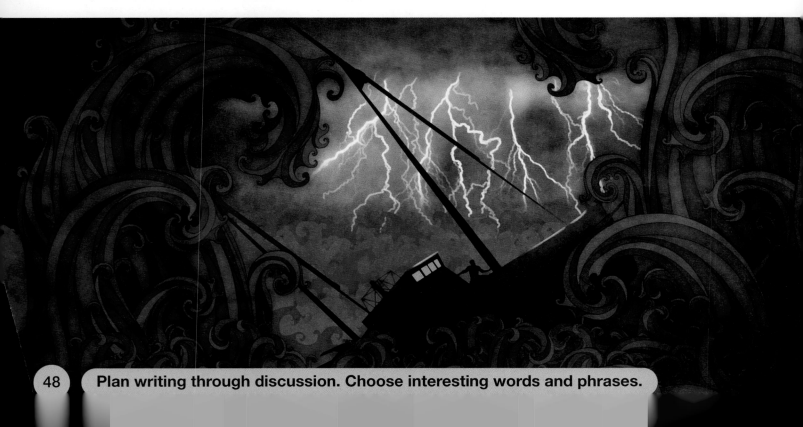

    Plan writing through discussion. Choose interesting words and phrases.

Reading and writing

The story is in three parts.
Beginning – before Jean threw the spear.
Middle – what happened after he threw the spear.
End – what happened after Jean made a promise.

❶ Write the sentences under the correct headings.

beginning   middle   end

- The knight carried Jean down to the bottom of the sea.
- The knight took him back to the boat.
- Jean hurled a spear.
- The storm died down.
- Jean removed the spear.
- The dolphin dived beneath the waves.
- Jean and his friends were fishing.

❷ What did Jean promise to do?

❸ Write the words that best describe a promise:

- something that you might be able to do
- something that you will do.

❹ Work in pairs. Talk about the questions.

- What things have you promised to do?
- Did you always keep your promise?
- Should you make a promise if you might not be able to keep it?

Sequence events in a story with beginning, middle and end.

Reading

Work with a partner and read about dolphins.

Listening and speaking

Talk about:

- the different ways that humans can cause dolphins harm
- how oil can injure or kill dolphins.

Writing

Design a poster giving information about an event that your class is organising to raise money for a dolphin conservation charity.

Dolphins

Dolphins are mammals that live in the ocean.

They are often injured or even killed by humans. Sometimes they get tangled in fishing nets. Sometimes they are killed for food or bait.

The most serious threat to dolphins is pollution.

Oil spills caused by underwater drilling or a ship running aground can cause dolphins to die.

- Oil can cover the dolphin's blowhole and enter its lungs, making it difficult to breathe.
- Oil can get into the dolphin's eyes, causing damage and even blindness.
- Oil can enter the dolphin's mouth. The dolphin can swallow it and damage its internal organs.

Factual information. Simple organisational devices.

6 Staying safe

World's Deadliest Creatures

Written by Anna Claybourne

Contents

Read the contents page and answer the questions.

1 What will you find out about in this book?

2 What is the title of the book?

3 What kind of book is it?

4 Who wrote the book?

5 There is no illustrator's name. Why do you think this is?

6 What will you find out about on page 6?

7 What will you find out about on page 10?

8 On what page will you find out about staying safe?

Reading

Look at the pictures and read the information on pages 52 to 54.

1 Deadly or not?

golden poison dart frog

dangerous!

whale shark

2

blue-ringed octopus

dangerous!

giant huntsman spider

horned lizard

hellbender

Which are the deadliest creatures in the world? Some look dangerous, but they are not. Others look safe, but watch out!

3

Australia

This funnel-web spider has deadly **venom** in its big fangs.
It can even bite through soft shoes.

4

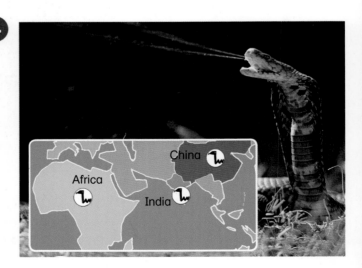

China

Africa

India

A spitting cobra can spit its venom two metres. It aims venom at your eyes, which can cause blindness.

Read aloud with increased accuracy, fluency and expression.

5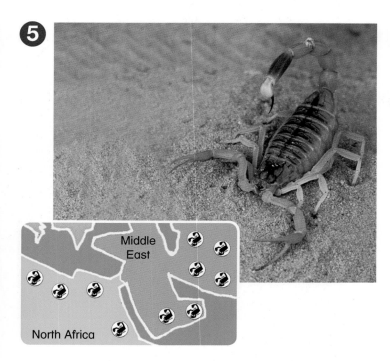

Deathstalker scorpions
hide in dark places.
They sting with their tails.

6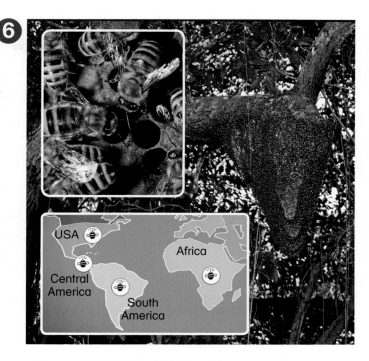

Over 20,000 killer bees can
swarm together.
Each bee has a very sharp sting.

7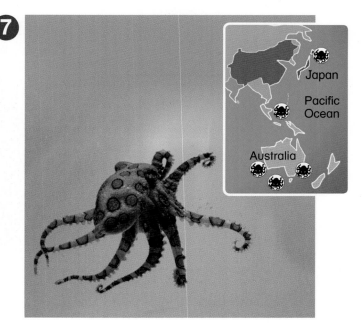

The blue-ringed octopus
has a venomous beak.
Its bite is deadly.

8

Tiger sharks often swim close
to beaches, so sometimes they
attack humans.
Their teeth and jaws are strong
enough to bite you in half.

9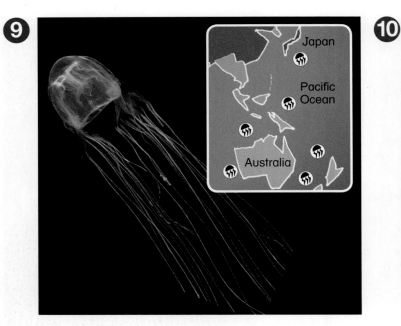

The box jellyfish has long, venomous **tentacles**.
Its venom can kill a human in three minutes.

10

The most **poisonous** creature in the world is the golden poison dart frog. It's deadly to eat, or even to touch.

11

If you see a dangerous animal like the ones in this book, keep away.

12

Most animals will **not** attack you, unless you bother them. Always treat animals with respect.

Read aloud with increased accuracy, fluency and expression.

Read the pages. Answer the questions.

Page 1
- Which creature is dangerous?
- Which creature is not dangerous? How can you tell?

Page 2
- Which creature is labelled 'dangerous'?

Page 3
- How does the funnel-web spider kill its prey?
- In what country is the funnel-web spider found?

Page 4
- How could a spitting cobra hurt you?
- In what countries are spitting cobras found?

Page 5
- How could the scorpion hurt you?
- In what countries are deathstalker scorpions found?
- Where do deathstalker scorpions hide?

Page 6
- What is a swarm of bees?
- How many killer bees can be in a swarm?
- In what countries are killer bees found?

Reading and writing

❶ Read pages 52 to 54 again to find out about dangerous creatures that live in water.

❷ Copy and complete the sentences.

tiger shark

blue-ringed octopus

box jellyfish

- The _____ has a venomous beak.
- The _____ sometimes attack humans.
- The _____ has long venomous tentacles.

Listening and speaking

People need water. Work with a partner and talk about why people need water.

Writing

❶ Write three things that people need water for.

❷ Draw a picture to show one thing that people need water for. Write a caption under it.

Find factual information. Organisational devices.

	bites	spits	stings
spider	✓		
cobra		✓	
scorpion			✓
octopus	✓		
bee			✓
shark	✓		

❶ Read the chart to find the answers.

- Does a cobra bite, spit or sting?
- Which creatures bite their prey?
- Which creatures sting their prey?

❷ Write a list of animals that are not safe to touch.

❸ Write a list of animals that are safe to touch.

Sounds and spelling

❶ One syllable is missing from a word in each sentence. Add the missing syllables. Copy the sentences.

- The funnel-web spi_____ has venom in its fangs.
- The spitting cob_____ can spit its venom two metres.
- The scor__on stings with its tail.
- The oc_____pus has a venomous beak.
- The box jel__fish has long tentacles.

com/pu/ter

❷ Add the missing syllable to complete each month. Write the names of the months correctly.

Jan/___/ar/y
Feb/ru/___/y
_____
Ap/_____
_____
_____
Ju/_____
Au/_____
Sep/_____/ber
Oc/to/_____
___/vem/ber
De/_____/ber

Identify syllables and split.

Sounds and spelling

❶ Write the words in rhyming groups under each heading.

> head   bear   beach   thread   tear   teach   reach   read   wear

sounds like 'peach'   sounds like 'bread'   sounds like 'pear'

   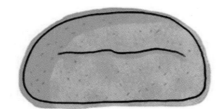

Listening and speaking

Read the sentences in the box. Work with a partner and talk about:

- the underlined words in the sentences.
- how you know how to pronounce each underlined word.

> The black car is in the <u>lead</u> in the race.
> I <u>read</u> my library book last night.

Sounds and spelling

Use the underlined words in the box above to complete these rhymes. Write the rhymes.

❶ _____ rhymes with head.

❷ _____ rhymes with bead.

Speaking and listening

1 **Work in pairs. Talk about the pictures.**

a

DANGER
KEEP OUT

b

c

BEWARE
FALLING ROCKS

d

e

DANGER
DEEP WATER

f

2 **Write sentences to tell about the dangers shown in each picture.**

Plan writing. Choose interesting words and phrases.

7 When Arthur Wouldn't Sleep

Follow in your book as you listen to the story.

"Come ON, Flora," Arthur said.
"Let's play jumping."

"Ssssh!" Flora mumbled. "It's bedtime.
Time to go to sleep."

The butterflies weren't sleeping, the bees
were busy buzzing and the grasshoppers
were jumping all over the place.

"I don't want to go to sleep," grumbled
Arthur.

Arthur gazed up at the clouds.

The more he gazed, the more funny
shapes he saw.

Then he started feeling very light.

Slowly, he started going up and up
and UP.

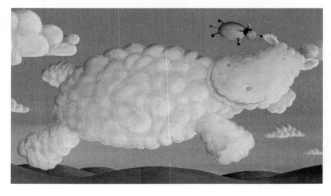

Soon he met a hippo.

"Where do you want to go?" the
hippo asked.

"I want to go where no one goes to
sleep," Arthur said.

And off they flew.

4

"This is your stop," said the hippo.

A ladybird was waiting for Arthur.

"Come with me," said the ladybird. "But don't forget. No sleeping!"

5

Soon they arrived at a party.

What a party!

"It's time for the Amazing Crazylegs Dancing Competition," the grasshopper said.

6

They danced and jumped …
Arthur joined in too.

The ladybird bounced, the sheep pranced and the grasshopper skipped and hopped and twirled.

Read aloud with increased accuracy, fluency and expression.

7

They jumped and danced … until their legs felt like jelly and they couldn't dance another step.

Who was going to win the Amazing Crazylegs Dancing Competition?

8

The grasshopper said, "… and the winner is …

ARTHUR! Do another dance, Arthur!"

But Arthur was very sleepy.

"I have to go now," he said. "I've got to tell Flora that there's a place where no one goes to sleep."

9

Off he flew, over the fields and back to Flora.

But Arthur didn't tell Flora about the place where no one goes to sleep …

10

… because in the morning, he'd forgotten all about it.

Reading and writing

1 Write the name of the main character in the story.

2 Write the names of the creatures that Arthur met at the Crazylegs Dancing Competition.

3 Choose the correct words to complete the sentences. Copy the sentences.

> busy buzzing   gazed   started going   started feeling   jumping

- The bees were _____.
- The grasshoppers were _____.
- Arthur _____ up at the clouds.
- He _____ very light.
- Slowly he _____ up and up and up.

4 Read page 61 again. Write the sentences that are true.

- Arthur was playing with Flora.
- Arthur was falling asleep
- The hippo was a cloud shape.
- Arthur saw a square shape.
- Arthur met a real hippo.
- The hippo was in Arthur's dream.

Find answers to questions by reading a section of text.

Spelling: suffixes

A suffix is a set of letters added to the end of a word.

For example:

Slow**ly** he started going up and up and UP.

Slow + **ly** = slowly

–ly is a suffix.

1 **Add the suffix –ly to change each word.**

smart + ly	quick + ly	lone + ly
slow + ly	calm + ly	like + ly
friend + ly	smooth + ly	love + ly
bright + ly	loud + ly	nice + ly

2 **Copy and complete the sentences, using the correct word.**

- The car drove _____ along the street. (slow, slowly)
- The car is very _____. (slow, slowly)
- I hope you have a _____ journey. (safe, safely)
- He crossed the road _____. (safe, safely)
- She is a good _____. (friendly, friend)
- He is a _____ boy. (friendly, friend)

3 **Choose two words from question 1 and write a sentence using each one.**

1 Choose the correct answer.

- Who gazed at the clouds?   Flora   Arthur
- Who met a hippo?   Arthur   sheep
- Who was waiting for Arthur?   ladybird   grasshopper

2 Write the two shorter words that make each compound word.

grasshopper   ladybird   butterfly   Crazylegs

3 Why does the word 'Crazylegs' have a capital letter at the beginning?

Reading and talking

"Ssssh!" Flora mumbled. "It's bedtime. Time to go to sleep."

"I don't want to go to sleep," grumbled Arthur.

1 Why do you think Flora mumbled?

2 Why do you think Arthur grumbled?

Reading and writing

1 **Read what happened at the Amazing Crazylegs Dancing Competition. Write a list of the verbs.**

They danced and jumped ... Arthur joined in too.

The ladybird bounced, the sheep pranced and the grasshopper skipped and hopped and twirled.

2 **Copy and complete the sentences telling friends what they will be able to do at the Amazing Crazylegs Dancing Competition.**

| prance | hop | jump | dance | bounce | twirl | skip |

- You can _____ and _____.
- You can _____ like the ladybird and _____ like the sheep.
- You can _____ and _____ and _____ like the grasshopper.

3 **Add the suffix –ed to make new words. Write the words.**

| rush | play | pull | jump | push |

4 **Choose two of the words and write a sentence for each.**

Writing

1 **Copy and complete the sentences. Use the words in the box.**

| moaned | yelled | asked | answered | whispered |

- "Can I have a biscuit?" _____ Tom.
- "I don't want to go," _____ Zen.
- "Ssssh! The baby is sleeping," _____ Mum.
- "I don't want to," she _____ at the top of her voice.
- "I am going to the shops," _____ Alisha.

2 **Choose two of the words from the box above and write a sentence for each.**

Speaking and listening

**This is a verse from a traditional African lullaby.
Learn the verse so that you can recite it from memory.**

The Moon-Baby

There's a beautiful golden cradle
That rocks in the rose-red sky;
I have seen it there in the evening air
Where the bats and beetles fly,
With little white clouds for curtains
And pillows of fleecy wool,
And a dear little bed for the moon-baby's head,
So tiny and beautiful.

Simple inferences. Vocabulary choices. Attentive listening.

Sounds and spelling

1 Read the sentence. Write the words with the letter _c_ that sounds like _s_.

- They danced and bounced and pranced at the place where no one sleeps.

2 Use the letters in the box to make rhyming words.

| l | d | p | m | r | n |

face   price
_ace   _ice

Reading and writing

1 Change the underlined words in the sentences for one of the words in the box. Write the new sentences.

| crazy | gazing | amazing |

- The little boy was <u>staring</u> at the monkeys playing.
- He took <u>awesome</u> photographs at the competition.
- She had a <u>wacky</u> hairstyle at the fancy dress party.

2 Write the words in the box in alphabetical order.

3 Write the words in the box again. Mark the syllables. Write the number of syllables in each word.

Reading and writing

1 Read the captions.

Meet new friends.

Fly there by hippo.

Prizes to be won.

Dance in the Amazing Crazylegs Dancing Competition.

An amazing place.

Don't forget: no sleeping.

Fantastic music.

Listen to the amazing Crazylegs Dance Band.

2 Design a poster for the Amazing Crazylegs Dancing Competition.

Speaking and listening

Work in pairs. Imagine you are interviewing Arthur about the Amazing Crazylegs Dancing Competition.

- One of you should imagine you are Arthur and the other a reporter from the local newspaper.

Writing

Write a newspaper report for your local newspaper about the Amazing Crazylegs Dancing Competition.

Use a variety of simple organisational devices in non-fiction. Write using a variety of sentence types.

8 The Pot of Gold

1 Work with a partner. Look at the front cover of the book and talk about:

- the characters' appearance
- how you think they are feeling
- what they are wearing
- any other information you can get from the front cover.

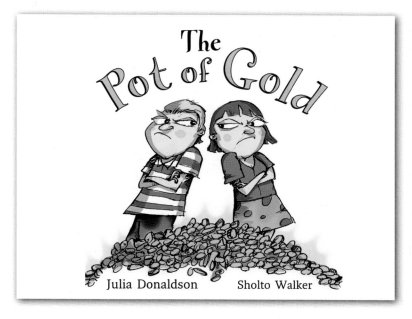

2 Work with a partner. Read the 'blurb' from the back cover of the book and talk about the questions.

- What do you think is going to happen in the story?
- What part might the little man have in the story?

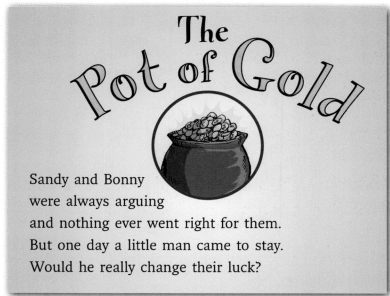

Sandy and Bonny
were always arguing
and nothing ever went right for them.
But one day a little man came to stay.
Would he really change their luck?

3 Now read the story with your partner. Take turns to read.

4 Who came to the door when the children were arguing?

The Pot of Gold

1

Sandy and Bonny kept sheep.

"Too many sheep," said Bonny.

"Not enough sheep," said Sandy.

The two of them were always arguing.

2

One evening, they were busy arguing when there was a tap at the door. There on the doorstep stood a little man. He wore a green hat and a ragged green coat. His green shoes had holes in the toes.

3

"Can I stay here for two nights?" he asked.

"Yes," said Sandy.

"No," said Bonny.

"I can pay," said the little man. He took two gold coins out of his pocket.

"Well?" he asked. "Can I stay?"

4

"Yes!" said Sandy and Bonny. For once they agreed about something.

They took him to his room.

"Good night, and good luck!" said the little man. Bonny laughed. "We never have any luck," she said. But she was wrong.

Read aloud with increased accuracy, fluency and expression.

5

The next day, Sandy was on the hill with the sheep when he saw a big pile of stones.

"That's funny," he said. "I can see something gleaming."

Sandy took away some of the stones, and he saw a heap of gold coins!

"I'll run home and fetch a big pot to carry them in," he said.

6

He started to run down the hill. But then he stopped.

"Suppose someone finds the coins when I'm gone?" he said to himself.

He put the stones back and stuck his stick into them, so that he would be able to find the right place again.

7

Sandy ran home. "We're rich!" he shouted. "Don't be so silly," said Bonny. But then Sandy told her about the gold coins. He grabbed a pot. "Let's go and get them!" he said.

8

"Don't be so silly," said Bonny again. "People will see us. Then everyone will want some of the gold."

"That's true," said Sandy. "Let's wait till it's dark."

9

Bonny put some food and water on the table.

"Just think," she said. "With all that money we can buy a new house."

"Don't be silly," said Sandy. "We don't need a new house. But we do need some more sheep."

10

"Sheep!" cried Bonny. "We've got too many sheep already. We can stop keeping sheep. And I can buy lots of new clothes."

"Clothes!" shouted Sandy. "You don't need any more clothes! You've got too many clothes already!"

He banged his fist on the table.

"I have not!" yelled Bonny. And she threw a chip at him.

"Missed!" shouted Sandy, and he threw some beans at her.

11

They were shouting so loudly that they didn't hear the little man come downstairs.

"Please could you stop making so much noise?" he asked.

12

"Oh, shut up!" yelled Bonny.

She was in such a bad mood that she picked up a jug of water and threw it all over the little man.

Sandy laughed.

Read aloud with increased accuracy, fluency and expression.

13

The little man gave them both a funny look. Then he went upstairs.

"Good night," he said. But this time he didn't say, "Good luck".

14

It was dark now and the moon was out. "Let's go and get the gold," said Sandy. They took the pot and carried it up the hill.

"There's the pile of stones with your stick in it," said Bonny.

She took away some of the stones. "I can't see any gold," she said. "You were just making it up!"

15

"No, I wasn't!" Sandy shouted. "I really did find a heap of gold coins." Then he spotted another pile of stones with a stick. "That's funny," he said.

Sandy and Bonny looked around them. There were hundreds of piles of stones, each one with a stick in it.

They hunted all night, but they didn't find the gold.

16

When they got home the little man had gone. But there were two gold coins on the table, and a note saying, "Keep looking".

Sandy and Bonny did keep looking. They looked every night. But they didn't find the gold.

They are still looking. And they are still arguing!

Writing

1 **Write a description of either Sandy or Bonny for a missing person poster.**

Sandy   Bonny

2 **Answer the questions.**

- What did Sandy and Bonny argue about?
- What time of day did they hear a tap at the door?
- Who tapped at the door?

3 **Write the adjectives that describe the old man and what he wore.**

There on the doorstep stood a little man. He wore a green hat and a ragged green coat. His green shoes had holes in the toes.

4 **Change the adjectives to make the man and his clothes different.**

5 **Draw the man you have described.**

Read and respond to questions. Vocabulary choices.

Reading and writing

Complete the sentences with the words that Sandy and Bonny said. Copy the sentences.

- "That's funny," he said. "_____ _____ ."

- "I'll run home _____ _____ ," he said.

- "Suppose someone "_____ _____ ?" he said to himself.

- "_____ !" he shouted.

- "_____ ," said Bonny.

- "_____ !" he said.

Speaking and listening

Work in pairs. Talk about a time when you argued with someone.

Writing

Write about the time you argued with someone.

❶ **Read pages 9–15 again. Write the sentences that are true.**

- Bonny didn't want to share the gold.
- Sandy agreed with Bonny about the gold.
- Bonny put some food and milk on the table.
- Sandy wanted to buy more sheep.
- Bonny wanted to buy new clothes.
- Sandy threw some beans before Bonny threw a chip.
- The little man was hungry so he came downstairs.
- Sandy laughed when Bonny threw water all over the little man.

❷ **Join the two sentences to make one sentence. Write the sentences.**

but   because   and

- "We can buy a new house. I can buy lots of new clothes."
- He banged his fist on the table. He was angry.
- The little man came downstairs. He heard loud shouting.
- The little man came downstairs. Sandy and Bonny didn't hear him.
- Bonny threw a jug of water all over the little man. Sandy laughed.

"Oh, shut up!" yelled Bonny.

She was in such a temper that she picked up a jug of water and threw it all over the little man.

Sandy laughed.

1 Copy and complete the sentences.

| argued | hunted | temper | gleaming | evening |

- He is in a bad _____ today.
- The children _____ over which game to play.
- The candle was _____ in the dark room.
- I went to visit my friend in the _____.
- He _____ for his lost keys.

2 Copy and complete the questions.

Who?   Why?

When?   **?**   How?

Where?   What?

- "<u>Why</u> did you choose a blue car?"
- "_____ rang the doorbell?"
- "_____ will we do today?"
- "_____ is the nearest supermarket?"
- "_____ will the film start?"
- "_____ many children are in the class?"

3 Write the compound words from question 2.

❶ Work with a partner and talk about:

- the story the pictures tell
- how Sandy and Bonny behaved
- what might have happened when the little man left.

❷ Write down words to describe Sandy and Bonny.

❸ Write a new story to match the pictures and tell what happened when the man left.

Use the structures of familiar stories in developing writing.

Reading and writing

① Match a word from each box to make pairs of words that have similar meanings. Write the words in pairs.

dangerous	trained	amusement
pleasure	prepared	hazardous

② Choose two words from question 1 and write a sentence for each.

③ Look at the first picture on page 82. List the clothing and equipment that the firefighters have.

Listening and speaking

Work with a partner. Look at the pictures on page 82 and talk about:

- the different places that firefighters put out fires
- the different places that fires could start on land
- things that might cause fires on land.

Writing

Write sentences to tell where firefighters put out fires. Illustrate one of the places and write a caption under it.

Reading and writing

Copy and complete.

Sirens _____ and lights _____ as the fire engine arrives.

The firefighters put out _____ with jets of _____ from _____ .

Speaking and listening

❶ Work with a partner and talk about:

- what can cause fires to start in houses
- what you should do if you notice a fire starting in a house.

❷ Work with a partner. Imagine one of you is making a phone call to report a fire and the other is receiving the call.

- Who would you phone?
- What number would you call?
- What information would you give?

Writing

❶ Write the telephone number that you would phone to report a fire.

❷ Write a list of the important things you would say when you phone to report a fire.

Attempt to express ideas precisely. Ways of speaking in different situations.

Reading and writing

❶ Copy and complete.

Fires spread quickly through
_____.

_____ water-bomb forest
fires.

Helicopters must _____ in
low.

The forests will _____
again.

❷ Copy and complete.

An oil well _____ can burn
like a huge, flaming _____.
This is called a _____.

Speaking and listening

Work in pairs. Talk about the questions.

- Why are oil well fires very dangerous to people?
- Why do fires spread quickly through forests?
- Why must the helicopters fly in low at a forest fire?

Reading and writing

① **Copy and complete.**

② **Write a description of the fire boat on page 83.**

> Firefighters use _____ to put out fires on small boats.
>
> Jet skis work in _____ water.
>
> Big oil _____ fires need fire boats with powerful _____.

Speaking and listening

Work with a partner and talk about:

- the picture of firefighters on a jet ski on page 83
- the firefighters' clothing and how it differs from a firefighter on land
- why it is different
- the ways the firefighters' equipment is different to equipment in a fire engine.

Features of text. Express ideas precisely.

Reading and writing

Index

❶ Answer the questions. Use the index to find the page where you will find the answer.

- What kind of fires need fire boats to put out the fire?
- How do helicopters put out forest fires?
- What kind of water do jet skis work in?
- Write the names of two types of fires where hoses are used.
- What warns people that a fire engine is coming?

❷ Choose two things from the index and write a sentence about each.

❸ Read the information about fire again.

- Write a title for a book that contains this information.
- Write headings for the different chapters in the book.

Listening and speaking

Work with a partner and talk about the pictures.

Why do you think this fire engine has a picture of an aeroplane on it?

Where would you park a fire engine at the airport? Why?

Where would you find fire hydrants?

What are they used for?

Writing

❶ Write a job advertisement for a firefighter.

- Include a list of facts about what a firefighter does.
- Illustrate the advertisement to make it attractive.

❷ Design and label a new piece of equipment for fighting fires in the future.

- Will it travel on land, in the air, at sea or will it be able to fight fires anywhere?

Text acknowledgements

The publishers gratefully acknowledge the permissions granted to reproduce copyright material in the book. Every effort has been made to contact the holders of copyright material, but if any have been inadvertently overlooked, the Publisher will be pleased to make the necessary arrangements at the first opportunity.

HarperCollins*Publishers* Limited; Fraser Ross for an extract and artwork from *Jodie the Juggler* by Vivian French, illustrated by Beccy Blake, text copyright © Vivian French. Joyce Vallar for the adapted poem 'Jason the Juggler', published in *Hector Hedgehog's Big Book of Rhymes*, copyright © Joyce Vallar; HarperCollins*Publishers* Limited; Caroline Sheldon for an extract and artwork from *Worm Looks for Lunch* by Julia Donaldson, illustrated by Martin Remphry, text copyright © Julia Donaldson; HarperCollins*Publishers* Limited; David Higham Associates for *Kind Emma* by Martin Waddell, illustrated by David Roberts, text copyright © Martin Waddell; Robert Charles Howard for the poem 'Dolphin Ballet' published in Unity Tree: *Collected Poems by Robert Charles Howard*, 2007, Createspace, copyright © Robert C. Howard; HarperCollins*Publishers*; Lucas Alexander Whitely Agency for *The Dolphin King* by Saviour Pirotta, illustrated by Fausto Bianchi, text copyright © Saviour Pirota; HarperCollins*Publishers* for *World's Deadliest Creatures* by Anna Claybourne, copyright © Anna Claybourne; HarperCollins*Publishers*; Catchpole Agency for *When Arthur Wouldn't Sleep*, written and illustrated by Joseph Theobald, copyright © Joseph Theobald; HarperCollins*Publishers*; Caroline Sheldon; Juliette Lott for *The Pot of Gold* by Julia Donaldson, illustrated by Sholto Walker, text copyright © Julia Donaldson; HarperCollins*Publishers* for *Fire! Fire!* by Maureen Haselhurst.

Photo acknowledgements
The publishers wish to thank the following for permission to reproduce photographs. Every effort has been made to trace copyright holders and to obtain their permission for the use of copyright materials. The publishers will gladly receive any information enabling them to rectify any error or omission at the first opportunity.

(t = top, c = centre, b = bottom, r = right, l = left)

Cover & p 1 David Roberts
p7 Larry Maurer/Shutterstock, p12t Blackboard1965/Shutterstock, p12rc Paolo Bona/Shutterstock, p12lc Pete Niesen/Shutterstock, p13t Sergei Bachlakov/Shutterstock, p13lc Mitch Gunn/Shutterstock, p13rc Galina Barskaya/Shutterstock, p13c Diego Barbieri/Shutterstock, p13b Neil Lang/Shutterstock, p14 Paolo Bona/Shutterstock, p16 Iurii Osadchi/Shutterstock, p18 A_Lesik/Shutterstock, p19 Suzanne Tucker/Shutterstock, p20 Kaliva/Shutterstock, p50 Igor Zh./Shutterstock, p51r Eric Isselee/Shutterstock, p51l DK Images, p52l inset imageBROKER/Alamy, p52tl Mirko Zanni/Getty Images, p52tr Michael Patrick O'Neill/Alamy, p52r inset Robert Pickett/PapillioPhotos, p52c inset Pat Morris/Ardea, p52rc Marcel van Kammen/Minden Pictures/FLPA, p52bl Nature Production/Naturepl, p55tc Digital Vision/Getty Images, p53tl Imagemore/Superstock, p53t inset ZoonarRF/Shutterstock, p53tr Fritz Polking/FLPA, p53bl DK Images, p53br James Watt/Photolibrary Group, p54tl ANT/Photoshot, p54tr imageBROKER/Alamy, p54bl Mark Moffett/Minden Pictures/FLPA, p54br Charles Hood/Photoshot, p55t Nature Production/Naturepl, p55tc Digital Vision/Getty Images, p55bc Imagemore/Superstock, p55b Fritz Polking/FLPA, p56l James Watt/Photolibrary Group, p56c DK Images, p56r ANT/Photoshot, p57l Ludmila Yilmaz/Shutterstock, p57r TTstudio/Shutterstock, p68 Claudio Divizia/Shutterstock, p81tl Imagetopshop/Alamy, p81tlc AAR Studio/Shutterstock, p81trc CandyBox Images/Shutterstock, p81tr Superstock, p81 UK: Photofusion Picture Library/Alamy, p81 USA: Gaetano/CORBIS, p81 Brazil: AFP/Getty Images, p81 Kenya: Sipa Press/Rex Features, p81 Australia: Anne Greenwood/Shutterstock, p81 Japan: Firepix International, p81 China: Firepix International, p81 India: Pacific Press/Getty Images, p82tl Firepix International, p82tc Naijlah Feanny-Hicks/Corbis, p82tr ChameleonsEye/Shutterstock, p82bl Isaiah Shook/Shutterstock, p82br Getty Images, p83tl Firepix International, p83lc Bruno Torres/Corbis, p83tr Andrea Booher/Wikimedia Commons, p83 inset Andrew Brown/Ecoscene/Corbis, p83bl ATG Ltd., p83bc Courtesy of NIST Intelligent Systems Division, p83br Automobiles Peugeot RC, p84 Gary L Jones/Shutterstock p85 ketmanee/Shutterstock, p86 Art Konovalov/Shutterstock, p87t Andrea Booher/Wikimedia Commons, p87b Getty Images, p88 Firepix International, p89 Imagetopshop/Alamy.